Also by Derek Wilson

East Africa Through a Thousand Years: A History

England in the Age of Thomas More

The People and The Book:
The Revolutionary Impact of the English Bible, 1380-1611

et Robin: A Biography of Robert Dudley, Earl of Leicester, 1533-1588

The Tower, 1078-1978

Tudor Tapestry: Men, Women and Society in Reformation England

White Gold: The Story of African Ivory

The World Encompassed: Drake's Great Voyage, 1577-1580

Rothschil

Swe

A